What do you call a stockbroker who's always right?

(See page 7)

What's the difference between a rooster and a salesman?

(See page 16)

How many used-car salesmen does it take to change a light bulb?

(See page 36)

What's the difference between a securities salesman and a pair of jockey shorts?

(See page 56)

What's the sexiest four-letter word to a salesman?

(See page 73)

Why is it easy to become a successful salesperson?

(See page 105)

## Also by Blanche Knott
## Published by St. Martin's Press

# Blanche Knott's
# Truly Tasteless
# $ALESMAN
# Jokes

**SMP**

**ST. MARTIN'S PAPERBACKS**

TRULY TASTELESS SALESMAN JOKES

Copyright © 1993 by Blanche Knott.

ISBN: 0-312-92978-1

Printed in the United States of America

St. Martin's Paperbacks edition/March 1993

10  9  8  7  6  5  4  3  2  1

For Michael, Leslie,
and Diana too

The sales manager went over the new rep's first expense report with special attention. "Let's see, gas a hundred and forty-five dollars, fine; entertainment moderate, fine; postage, of course; accommodation, very reasonable . . . What's this? One pair handmade Italian shoes, a hundred and eighty dollars! John, is this some kind of a joke?"

"It's no joke, Mr. McCormack. I wore out my shoes walking around my territory and I needed a new pair."

"That's what your salary's for," reprimanded the sales manager. "Items like that do *not* belong on your expense account." He crossed out the offending item, reduced the total accordingly, initialed the report, and handed it back. "Pass it on to accounting."

After a second long sales trip, John returned to Mr. McCormack's office with his expenses. The sales manager nodded approvingly as he checked off the contents. "No Italian shoes in here this time, I see," he commented smugly as he handed the papers back.

"Oh, they're there all right," replied John. "Just try and find them."

•

The sales rep was stuck in a tiny town out in the middle of nowhere, waiting for a shipment to come in. One week stretched to two, and at the end of the second week he couldn't take it anymore. He went into the local whorehouse, plunked down $100, and requested the worst blow job in the joint.

Pocketing the cash, the madam said, "Sir, for one hundred dollars you don't need to settle for the worst. Why, it'll buy you the very best we have to offer."

"Let me set you straight," explained the salesman. "I'm not horny, just homesick."

•

Two salesmen were comparing notes over lunch one day. "So, has the recession had an effect on your door-to-door sales?" asked Eric.

"I'll say," answered Ron gloomily. "I find twice as many husbands at home."

●

The super-salesman arrived at the Pearly Gates at the same time as a flashy dude from Harlem. "Welcome to Heaven," said St. Peter warmly. "I'm in such a good mood today that I'm going to offer both of you whatever your heart desires. What would you like, sir?" he asked, turning to the black guy.

The fellow considered for a moment, then said, "I'd like a million bucks."

In an instant his arms were filled with cash, and he walked through the Pearly Gates with a smile a mile wide.

"And you, sir?" asked St. Peter, turning to the legendary salesman.

"I'd like twenty bucks worth of fake gold jewelry," he responded instantly, "and ten minutes alone with that dude."

●

The company's top salesman was trying to appease his wife, who was infuriated by how little time he spent at home. "Tell me what you want, Louise," he begged. "Nothing's too good for you. How about a new Cuisinart?"

She shook her head.

"A mink? Floor length, this time?"

Her pout deepened.

"A two-week Caribbean cruise?"

She shook her head more vehemently.

"A ski chalet? Or maybe a place at the beach?"

Still no.

"So what *do* you want, Louise?" asked the frustrated salesman.

"A divorce."

"Gee," he admitted, "I wasn't planning to spend *that* much."

•

The irate customer marched into the men's clothing store and sought out the salesman who had helped him. "Remember this buttondown jacket you sold me last week?" he demanded. "Look—it burst at the seams!"

"Sure shows how well the buttons were sewn on," the salesman pointed out thoughtfully.

•

The two dimwitted salesmen decided to make a little extra money on weekends, so they rented a truck, drove out to the country, and filled it with watermelons at a dollar apiece. They drove back into the city and set up shop on the street corner selling melons for a dollar. To their delight they sold the whole truckful within two hours. But when they counted up their cash, they were shocked and disappointed to realize they had merely broken even.

After much figuring and headscratching, one salesman turned to the other and said accusingly, "See? I told you we should have rented a bigger truck."

•

A sales rep arrived at a country store and asked the new clerk, "Betsy, do you know the difference between a Caesar Salad and a blow job?"

"No," she replied.

"Great! Let's have lunch."

•

A door-to-door encyclopedia salesman and his two trainees show up at a farmhouse one afternoon, and the kindly farmer agrees to buy a set of books from the tenacious salesman. But all three have to promise not to touch his virginal daughter while he goes to the bank to get the money.

When the farmer returns, he finds all three salesmen in bed with her. Irate, he fires a shotgun blast over their heads, marches them out to the garden, and tells them each to pick ten of any fruit or vegetable.

The first trainee comes forward with ten peas. "Shove them up your ass," the farmer orders. The second trainee turns up with ten tomatoes and gets the same order. He has some trouble getting them up his ass, especially since he keeps cracking up, but he finally gets the job done.

"You're free to go," the farmer says to him, "but do you mind if I ask what's so damn funny?"

Collapsing with laughter once again, the sales trainee says, "Our boss is still out there, picking watermelons!"

•

When a company fell on hard times, the sales manager was asked to lay off two of his sales-people. The decision came down to Jack and Jill, both of whom were equally honest and dedicated to their jobs. Unable to choose which one to fire, the sales manager arbitrarily decided that the first to leave his or her desk the next day would be the one to get the ax.

The next morning found Jill at her desk, rubbing her temples. Asking Jack for some aspirin, she headed to the water cooler and that's when the sales manager caught up with her.

"I've got some bad news, Jill," he said. "I'm going to have to lay you or Jack off."

"Jack off," she snapped. "I have a headache."

"Can I help you, ma'am?" asked the furniture salesman politely.

"Yeah. I'm looking for a sexual sofa," she replied.

"Uh . . . I think you must mean a *sectional* sofa," corrected the salesman, blushing.

"Nope, I know what I want," said the customer bluntly. "See, my boyfriend wants an occasional piece in the living room."

•

What do you call a stockbroker who's always right?

Under indictment.

•

The manager of a ladies' dress shop realized it was time to give one of her sales clerks a little talking-to. "Tina, your figures are well below any of our other salespeople's. In fact, unless you can improve your record by the end of the month, I'm going to have to let you go."

"I'm sorry, Mrs. Garcia," said a chastened

Tina. "Can you give me any advice on how to do better?"

"Well, there's an old trick I can tell you about. It sounds silly, but it's worked for me in the past. Get hold of a dictionary and go through it page by page until you come to a word that has particular power for you. Memorize it, work it into your sales pitch whenever it seems appropriate, and you'll be amazed at the results."

Sure enough, Tina's figures went way up, and at the end of the month, Mrs. Garcia called her in again and congratulated her. "Did you try my little trick?" she asked.

Tina nodded. "It took me the whole weekend to find the right word, but I did: 'fantastic.' "

" 'Fantastic.' What a good word," commented Mrs. Garcia. "How have you been using it?"

"Well, my first customer on Monday was a woman who told me her little girl had just been accepted into the most exclusive prep school in the city. I said, 'Fantastic.' She went on to tell me about how her daughter always got straight As, was captain of the swim team, and was the most popular girl in her class but was always home in bed by eleven at night. I said, 'Fantastic.' And she bought three dresses, two blouses, a skirt, and a sweater set. My next customer told me she needed a formal dress for the spring ball at the Ardsley Country Club, which she was in charge of. I said, 'Fantastic.' She went on to say that ten other women had wanted to head the dance committee but she had won because her tennis game was the best, she had the best figure, and her husband made the most money. I said, 'Fantastic.' And she not only bought a designer gown but three pairs of shorts, two hats, and a raincoat. And it's been like that all week: the customers keep boasting, I keep saying 'Fantastic', and they keep buying."

"Excellent work, Tina," complemented her boss. "Just as a point of interest, what was it you used to say to customers before you discovered your power word?"

Tina shrugged. "Huh? Oh, just 'Who gives a shit?'"

•

Two buyers were talking shop one day. "You ever deal with the rep from Supreme Furs?" asked one.

"I sure do," he replied. "And I gotta say she is the most tight-fisted, cutthroat aggressive bitch I've encountered since I went into this business."

"So why keep dealing with her?"

"Because she's great in bed."

•

What's the difference between a really great sales force and a flock of vultures?

Vultures don't get Christmas bonuses.

Another difference?

Vultures' wingtips don't come off.

•

LaBonia was an experienced salesman whose territory included some rough neighborhoods. One evening he was heading home later than usual when two hoods came up behind him, threatened him with a gun, and demanded all his money.

Sighing deeply, LaBonia emptied his wallet of some $300 in cash. Then, nonchalantly, he pulled out his own gun and extracted $6 from the wad of bills.

"What the hell?" asked the puzzled robber.

"Listen, buddy," the salesman pointed out in a reasonable tone, "you can't tell me you're gonna refuse a two percent discount on an all-cash transaction."

•

Sales at the Acme Office Supplies were pretty slow, and old Mr. Acme finally realized it was probably time to offer his sales force a little bit of an incentive. So he gathered them all together and announced a wonderful new bonus plan.

"Here's how it's going to work: next season, every rep who increases orders by twenty percent gets a yellow certificate. Every rep who increases sales by forty percent gets a blue certificate. And everyone who increases their orders by fifty percent or more gets a badge!" he announced proudly.

"What's the badge say?" asked someone from the back of the room.

"Why . . . it says the owner of this badge has a yellow and a blue certificate."

•

"I figured that salesman for a crook from the minute he walked in here," muttered the buyer. "I knew I should never have trusted him."

"Why not?"

"Because when he left, he shook hands with me."

"So?"

"Now I'm missing a finger!"

•

Definition of a buyer: someone who knows more and more about less and less until finally they know everything about nothing.

Definition of a rep: someone who knows less and less about more and more until at the end they know nothing about anything.

●

A rep for a small manufacturing company was in the field when a tremendous storm front caught up with him and all outbound flights were canceled. He cabled the home office: MAROONED BY FLOODS. SEND INSTRUCTIONS.

The owner of the firm, a woman of legendary tightfistedness, wired back: BEGIN ANNUAL VACATION IMMEDIATELY.

●

Fred wanted to start his own business, so he saved his money and opened a sex boutique. After a week or so, his friend Morris dropped in and asked how things were going.

Fred conceded that things had been slow the first few days. "I sold a few bits of lingerie, a couple of French ticklers. But the last few days, dildoes have really been moving."

"No kidding?" asked Morris.

"Yeah," Fred went on. "I was even starting to run low when this really nearsighted dyke demanded the red plaid model with a silver rim."

"So what'd you do?"

"Sold her my thermos."

•

How could you tell the Wall Street broker was into S&M?

She got off on municipal bonds.

•

A travelling salesman is staying in a futuristic motel. He has an important sales call the next morning, and realizing he needs a trim, he calls the desk clerk to inquire whether there's a barber on the premises. "I'm afraid not, sir," replies the clerk, "but down the hall there's a bank of vending machines, and one will give you a haircut." Thoroughly intrigued, the salesman finds the machine, inserts fifty cents, and sticks his head in the opening. The machine starts buzzing and whirring. Fifteen seconds later he pulls out his head and discovers he's gotten the best haircut of his life.

Two feet away is another machine that says MANICURES FIFTY CENTS, and the salesman thinks,

Why not? So he pays the money, inserts his hands into the slot, and out they come looking terrific.

The next machine has a big sign: THIS MACHINE DOES WHAT MEN NEED MOST WHEN AWAY FROM THEIR WIVES. The salesman looks both ways, unzips his fly, inserts his dick, and puts in fifty cents. The machine buzzes away as the guy screams in excruciating pain. Fifteen seconds later it stops and he pulls it out with trembling hands.

There's a button sewed to the tip.

●

Two salesmen's wives were comparing notes. "Lou's always bringing home samples, and I love it," sighed one. "The cutest clothes, and he always knows my size."

"Yeah, well, Jim's always bringing home samples too, and it makes me mad as hell," complained the other.

"No kidding? What kind of business is he in?"

"He signs up girls for a model agency."

●

Rachel decided to celebrate her promotion to Vice President by buying a new car. She really wanted a BMW, but she admitted to the salesman that they were more expensive than she could afford.

"Hang on, Miss—I think I have just the car for you," said the salesman, sounding excited. He led her over to a beautiful charcoal grey 320i which looked and ran as though it were brand-new. In fact, it only had 5,712 miles on it.

"What's the deal here?" asked Rachel suspiciously. "Either the mileage is false or something's radically wrong with this car."

The salesman assured her that it was in perfect working order, and that he would provide a 50,000-mile warranty to prove it.

"You mean the owner just traded it in after only five thousand-plus miles?"

The salesman nodded. "He was *very* picky."

"So what was wrong with it?" she asked.

"The ashtrays were full."

•

The priest organized a weekend camping retreat for his church group. As luck would have it, no sooner had everyone set up their tents than the skies opened up with a downpour. It poured all night and continued to rain steadily throughout the day on all the bedraggled campers.

Finally one of them turned to the priest. "Gee, Father O'Hare, can't you do something about this weather?"

The priest shook his head. "Sorry, I'm in sales, not management."

●

A book lover, Betty frequently consulted the staff at her local bookshop for their recommendations. But she was highly insulted when the clerk's suggestion one day was a book called *The Husband's Pal—Five Hundred Good Reasons to Explain Why You Stayed Out Late*.

"What makes you think this kind of junk would interest *me*?" she demanded.

"Because your husband picked up a copy this morning," replied the clerk gently.

●

What's the difference between a rooster and a salesman?

A rooster clucks defiance . . .

●

An old Jew was retiring from the string-and-twine business. "Herschel," he implored his best friend, "I got one last load of string. Buy me out so I can retire with an empty shop and a clear heart."

Herschel had no interest in purchasing a load of string, but his old friend's impassioned pleading finally wore him down. "All right, Myron, all right," he finally conceded. "I'll buy some of your string—enough to reach from the tip of your nose to the tip of your dick."

To Herschel's surprise, his friend embraced him warmly and left without another word. He was even more surprised when a truck arrived the next morning loaded with a massive roll of string. "Myron, what is this!" he screamed at his friend over the phone.

"My nose is in Palm Beach," explained Myron happily, "but the tip of my dick is buried somewhere outside Minsk."

•

Definition of a brush fire: what happens when a match drops on a Fuller man's samples.

•

A handsome sales rep had earned quite a reputation as a ladies' man. One of the advantages of travelling his far-flung rural territory was that he met lots of lonely farm women eager for a chance at romance. Of course a possessive farmer was usually part of the picture, but Eric considered himself quite an expert at getting around any such obstacles.

Late one day his car broke down on a back road in Amarillo County, and a passing rancher offered him a bed for the night. "But no funny business," warned his benefactor. "I have a nineteen-year-old daughter at home, and Loretta's my pride and joy."

"It wouldn't even cross my mind," Eric promised solemnly. "I'm a happily married man." He observed that Loretta was very attractive indeed, and from the look she shot him as she said goodnight, he figured the feeling was mutual.

Late that night the farmer was awakened by a peculiar noise. Grabbing his shotgun, he went down the hall to investigate and his worst fears were concerned: the noise was coming from Loretta's room. He threw open the door just in time to catch the salesman getting out of her bed, and he let him have it with the left barrel— right through his dick.

Eric let out an agonized scream and ran out of the house to his car. Clutching his injured genitals, faint with pain and fear, he drove the 60 miles to the nearest town and pounded on the door of the only clinic. A sleepy GP carefully examined his injuries in complete silence. Finally the doctor commented that he was truly in a mess and there wasn't much he could do for him. "Let me thing, señor . . . I could give you the name of a good man in El Paso," the doctor offered.

"Please help me, *please,*" begged Eric. "I'll go straight there. Is he a urologist? A surgeon?"

"Oh, he's not a specialist. Actually, he's not even a doctor," replied the doctor matter-of-factly. "He's a piccolo player, and he'll be able to show you where to put your fingers when you want to take a leak."

•

Two employees were marveling about the owner of the company's talents. "He's a sleazeball, no doubt about it," said Millie with a shrug, "but he's always figuring the angles on how to boost sales. He's never lost an opportunity to make money."

"That's for sure," agreed Dave. "Why, I was in his office when a guy from the Department of the Interior was raking him over the coals about all the acid rain his factories produce."

"So what'd he say?"

"He brightened right up and said, 'I'm glad you asked me that. Tomorrow morning my sales force will be introducing a whole new line of acid-resistant umbrellas."

•

What did the no-nonsense farmer's daughter say to the travelling salesman?
  "Till it like it is."

•

The eager-beaver insurance saleswoman was sure she could clinch the sale with this demonstration of her policy's extra benefits. "Say you fall off the observation deck of the World Trade Center," she proposed enthusiastically. "If you hit the ground, we pay you double indemnity. Plus, you get three hundred and forty-four dollars a week for as long as you live. And payment begins from the second you're in the air, so you're even making money on the way down."

•

What do you call someone who sells RVs?
  A wheel estate dealer.

•

Sandy was delighted to get a summer job working in the corner grocery store. She'd only been on the job a few days when a very snooty customer walked in and demanded half a cabbage.

"I'm sorry, ma'am," said Sandy politely, "but I'm not allowed to cut the produce up like that."

"Young lady, I have no need for a whole cabbage and see no reason why I should be forced to pay for one. I insist that you cut one in half for me immediately."

"I'd like to oblige you, but, you see, it's against store policy—" Sandy explained.

"I can't believe anyone as young and inexperienced as you would know the first thing about store policy," interrupted the customer nastily.

"Just one moment, please," muttered Sandy, and went off to find the manager at his desk. "Mr. Neff, I'm sorry to bother you, but there's a major asshole out in the produce department who wants to buy half a cabbage . . ." Just then, out of the corner of her eye, Sandy noticed that the obnoxious customer had followed her back, and continued, "and this nice lady would like to buy the other half."

•

Two salesmen were chatting over lunch when Gary said he'd had to fire his secretary that morning. "She was two hours late. Can you believe it?"

"Mine was late, too," said Ben, "but I gave her a big raise."

"What on earth for?" asked Gary.

"She was two months late," explained Ben.

•

"Do you talk to your wife while you're having sex?" asked one sales associate of another.

He shook his head. "Nope—but I would if I could reach the phone."

•

The would-be homeowner was tired of being dragged from pillar to post, being shown houses that cost substantially more than he could afford. Finally he confronted the real-estate agent. "You're wasting my time," he accused her bluntly. "Can't you show me something in the price range I gave you in the first place?"

"Actually, yes," she replied sharply, "but if I were to sell it to you, I'd have to make a basset hound homeless."

•

Approaching eighty-five years of age, Mrs. Lipkowitz finally decided it was time to give up her apartment in New York and move to Miami. She was given the name of a Florida realtor, who enthusiastically drove her all over Miami, extolling the virtues of every apartment they looked at.

"And this one, what a steal," he rhapsodized, "the investment of a lifetime. Why, in ten years it's gonna be worth three times—"

"Sonny," interrupted Mrs. Lipkowitz, "at my age I don't even buy green bananas."

●

What do you call it when a sales rep gets pregnant at an office party?

A desk job.

●

A sales rep got stuck in bumper-to-bumper traffic in a bad part of town. Then the car stalled and he couldn't get it to start again. Cursing, he pushed it to the side of the street and opened the hood to see if he could figure out the problem. While he was poking away, he heard a funny noise from the other side of the car. Going round to investigate, he saw a ghetto kid squatting by his back wheel.

Flashing him a big smile and a wink, the kid said, "No problem, buddy. You get the battery and I'll take the hubcaps."

·

What's the definition of a good salesperson?

Someone who can make a living going from door to door selling signs that read NO SALESPEOPLE ALLOWED.

·

Part of a certain Avon lady's territory included a ten-story high-rise apartment complex, and she had a favorite customer on the eighth floor. While on her way out of the elevator, the Avon lady realized she was about to fart. Looking around and not finding any place more appropriate, she darted back into the empty elevator and relieved herself. The aroma was particularly deadly, so she rummaged through her Avon sample bag until she came across some pine-scented spray, with which she liberally doused the elevator.

By this time the elevator was back on the ground floor, and when the doors opened a drunk reeled in. Trying to look nonchalant, the Avon lady started to push by him, but the drunk kept sniffing around and eyeing her suspiciously.

"Is something wrong, sir?" she asked stiffly.

"Well I don't know about you, lady," said the drunk, "but it smells like someone took a shit on a Christmas tree in here!"

•

Two salesmen were writing up their orders when the conversation came around to last night's big date. "So, how'd it go, Harry?" asked Gil.

"Terrible," admitted Harry. "The moment we got back to her place the phone started ringing. There must have been fifteen calls from guys wanting to ask her out. It never stopped, and we never got started."

Gil tried to comfort him. "It could be worse, Harry. After all, an attractive young woman's allowed to have her number in the phone book, now isn't she?"

"Yeah, but not in the Yellow Pages."

•

Why did the gay salesman keep getting fired?
He blew every sales opportunity.

The door-to-door salesman was doing nicely until his main competitor put a bunch of fresh-faced schoolboys on the route. Business fell off sharply, and Wilcox was reduced to sitting on his butt trying to figure out how to get back on his feet. Finally he figured it out.

"Good morning, ma'am, I hope you can help me," he said to the woman who answered the next doorbell he rang. "I'm working my son's way through college."

•

Walking into a local bar, a salesman sees a very lovely young woman sitting only a few chairs down. He moves over and proceeds to engage her in conversation. Finally, confident of his successful track record as an effective salesman, he asks, "I know you think I'm pretty cute. Let's cut out the bullshit. You want to go out to a movie?"

She hauls off and slugs him so hard he lands on the floor. "Gee," he says, picking himself up and brushing himself off, "then I guess a blow job is out of the question too, huh?"

•

A panhandler working the Wall Street area approached a well-dressed salesman on his way to a big sales conference. "Sorry, buddy, but I never give money to anyone on the street," was his response.

"So what should I do," asked the panhandler, "come up to your office?"

•

Hersch was a salesman. One day as he was driving across the Negev desert he spotted what looked like a body by the side of the road. Hersch slammed on the brakes, ran over, and discovered an Arab on the brink of death. Hersch took the poor man into his arms and bent close so he could make out his parched whisper.

"Water, *effendi* . . . water."

"Are you in luck!" cried Hersch exultantly. "Why, right here in my carrying case, which is right here beside me, I happen to have the finest collection of one hundred percent silk neckties to be found this side of the King David Hotel. Normally thirty-five dollars, but for you, twenty-two fifty."

"Water, *effendi*, water," gasped the Arab, plucking feebly at Hersch's sleeve.

"I tell you what. Since you seem like such a nice guy, I'll make it two for thirty-five dollars—that's for a polysilk blend, though."

"Water, *effendi,* water."

"You drive a hard bargain." Hersch shook his head regretfully. "Okay, any tie you want for sixteen-fifty, but I can't go any lower."

"Water, *effendi,* water." The dying Arab's words were barely audible.

"Oh, it's *water* you want. Why didn't you say so?" asked Hersch. "Well, you're in luck again. Just over that sand dune's a lovely resort, used to vacation there myself. They'll give you all the water you want." And Hersch got back in his car and drove away.

The Arab managed to stagger to the top of the sand dune, and, sure enough, a neon-lit sign announcing *Le Club Gaza* was visible from the top. The Arab summoned the last of his strength, crawled across the burning sand to the entrance, and collapsed. "Water, *effendi.* Water," he croaked.

"Ah, you want water," said the doorman sympathetically. "We have all kinds: mineral water, well water, club soda, Perrier, seltzer. Only thing is, you have to have a tie to get in."

•

Why did the real-estate broker file for divorce?

He discovered his wife was selling lots on the side.

•

The investment counselor took a look at his new client's financial papers and pointed out that she was in a very high tax bracket. "I have an investment that might be just the thing for you," he proposed. "A movie tax shelter."

The client's eyes lit up with visions of hobnobbing with movie stars and visits to Hollywood. "Can you show me something about the project?" she wondered.

The fellow took a folder out of his drawer and handed it over. "It's a big-budget musical, starts filming in July. The write-offs are going to be tremendous."

"I see. But if it's a musical, how come the file's marked 'Science Fiction'?"

The investment counselor shrugged. "I file these deals according to the accounting methods used."

•

The train pulled out of Wichita, and the salesman was just nodding off when a woman in the upper berth leaned over and said she was cold. Flashing him a winning smile, she asked if he'd mind finding the porter and getting her another blanket.

"Tell you what," proposed the salesman. "Why don't we pretend we're married instead?"

"Well . . . okay," she replied, unsure what he meant.

"So we're married. Get your own goddamn blanket!"

•

What do you call a stockbroker with diarrhea?
  A Wall Street runner.

•

A shoe salesman took a fancy to one of the women at the front desk of his hotel and offered her $100 for an hour in his room. She assured him that she didn't do it for money, only for love. In any case, his crude come-on had ruined the possibility of any romantic feelings on her part.

Unfazed, the superconfident salesman mentioned that he sold designer shoes and had some terrific samples. So the woman came up to his room for a look and promptly fell in love with a pair of leopardskin pumps. "I don't get much of a kick out of sex with strangers," she said, "but you can give it your best shot." And she undressed and lay down on his bed.

Sure she couldn't resist his lovemaking skills, the salesman started pumping away, but she lay there like a dishrag. Not too much later, though, he felt one arm wrap around him, then one leg, then the other arm and the other leg. "Thought you wouldn't get worked up, eh?" he chortled smugly. "Best fuck you've ever had, now isn't it?"

"Oh, no, that's not it," she responded calmly. "I'm just trying on my new shoes."

•

Why was the hooker with leprosy hopping around on one foot?

When business got slow, she took twenty percent off.

•

"Man, that real-estate agent is just too sharp for me," groaned Barney to his buddy Joel. "I bought five acres of land that turned out to be underwater."

"So why didn't you get mad as hell?" asked Joel.

"I did, even made her come out and look it over with me . . . and next thing I know, she's selling me a motorboat."

•

"Great tip for you," enthused the stockbroker to a loyal client. "Really think you should take a strong position on this stock."

"How come?" asked the customer.

"Because I want to sell mine."

•

The door-to-door saleswoman could barely make herself heard to the woman who opened the door because of the ferocious barking of the three dogs inside the house. After several attempts to begin her spiel, each drowned out by the tremendous yapping, she shrugged, picked up her case, and headed back down the front walk.

"Hang on a sec!" called the homeowner to her surprise, closing the dogs in the house and following her down to the street. "I'm in sales myself, and I like to see a rep give it his best shot. I think you gave up awfully easily, don't you?"

"Frankly, no," replied the irritated saleswoman. "I'm selling burglar alarms."

•

The travelling salesman arrived home from a week on the road, kissed his wife, and asked, "How are the kids?"

"Well, honey, I've got some good news and some bad news," she replied. "The bad news is that Bill Jr. cut up Blair into little tiny pieces and used her for bait."

The salesman paled. "Jesus. What the hell's the *good* news?"

"The fish Bill Jr. caught were delicious."

•

When Felix, the regional sales manager for a machine tools company, got home from the office, his wife couldn't help noticing that his tie was loose, his fly unzipped, his hair dishevelled, he smelled of perfume, and his collar was covered with lipstick. "Rough day at the office?" she commented.

"Not too bad," he said nonchalantly. "Had to break in a new sales associate, but I think she'll work out."

"Does she take shorthand?" asked his wife.

"No," blurted Felix, "but she gives it."

•

A salesman used to supplement his income by gambling at poker, joining games wherever he happened to find himself. And he thought he'd seen it all, until he happened into a game in a little town in Tennessee and found himself seated next to a German Shepherd. A few hands later, the dog drew a straight flush and collected the jackpot.

"Unbelievable," exclaimed the salesman. "I've played a lot of cards in my day, but I never imagined I'd see a dog win at poker."

"Aaaa, he's not that hard to beat," said an old geezer at the table with a dismissive snort. "Every time he gets a good hand, he wags his tail."

•

When his new assistant came in on Monday morning, the divisional sales manager gave him a little speech about the company and the way it did business, concluding, "Remember, Hawkins —you can't cheat an honest man."

"Certainly not," agreed Hawkins, nodding earnestly.

"Luckily," continued the sales manager, "that's not the sort of clientele we cater to."

•

What's a sales manager's dream?

Finding out his assistant is pregnant—and her boyfriend's going to marry her.

•

A well-dressed fellow plunked down his two huge suitcases in front of a pleasant-looking woman on the commuter train and said, "Miss, I think you might be interested in a very special watch I happen to be selling."

The woman shook her head firmly. "I already have a watch, thanks."

"Ah, but you don't know what this watch can do," he pointed out enthusiastically. "Listen." He pushed a little button and a voice said clearly, "The time is six fifty-seven."

"Nice, but I don't need a watch," she said decisively.

"I quite understand, but just take a look at this." He pushed another little button and the dial turned into a tiny color television screen on which the evening news was coming through loud and clear.

"Impressive," admitted the woman, "but I already have a television."

"How about a Walkman?" The salesman unfolded little earphones from the watch strap, tuned the watch to the station of her choice, and watched her face as she listened to a passage from a Mozart concerto. Still, she handed it back, shaking her head regretfully.

"But that's not all," he continued, undeterred. "What's your home number?" He punched it into a tiny keypad, handed over the watch, and the woman found herself speaking to her house-keeper over a perfectly clear connection.

She was impressed. "Okay, how much is it?"

"Now there's the good news: you get a watch, a color television, a portable radio, and a cellular phone, all for only one eighty-nine ninety-five."

"All right," she said, "I'll buy one."

Taking her money, the salesman shook her hand, assured her she'd made a wise choice, and headed down the aisle. "Wait!" she called out. "You forgot your sample cases!"

"Those aren't sample cases," he called back. "They're the batteries for the watch."

•

How many used-car salesmen does it take to change a light bulb?

Three. One to change the bulb, and two to try and kick the chair out from underneath him.

•

One typically windy Chicago winter afternoon Pete came out to keep his friend Paul company selling newspapers on the street corner. "Jeez, Paulie, I don't know how you do it," he muttered, teeth chattering. "Five minutes out here and I'm already half frozen."

Paul grinned. "Doesn't bother me, Pete. See, selling all these newspapers keeps up the circulation."

●

Definition of a salesperson: someone with a smile on his face, a firm handshake, and a lousy territory.

●

The salesperson at the Pink Pussycat boutique didn't bat an eye when the customer purchased an artificial vagina. "What're you going to use it for?" she asked.

"None of your business," answered the customer, thoroughly offended.

"Calm down, buddy, calm down," she soothed. "The only reason I'm asking is that if it's food, we don't have to charge you sales tax."

The salesman returned from his final Gamblers Anonymous meeting with the news that he was cured for good. "I'll never play the horses again, honey," he promised. "From now on, I'm putting our money safely in the stock market, where it belongs."

"That's wonderful, sweetheart," said his wife. "But are you sure you'll know what you're doing?"

"Of course I will," he enthused. "In fact I've already got it all figured out. I'm betting IBM to win, AT&T to place, and Exxon to show."

•

The flower vendor was an old hand at unloading his last few bunches. Appealing to a businessman on his way home, the vendor said, "How about a nice bunch of roses to surprise your wife?"

"Haven't got a wife," responded the businessman gruffly.

"Then how about some carnations for your girlfriend?" proposed the vendor without missing a beat.

"Haven't got a girlfriend."

"You lucky guy!" The vendor broke into a big smile. "Buy 'em both to celebrate!"

A salesman dies and goes to heaven, only to find a long, long line waiting at the Pearly Gates. He waits and waits for hours, talking to the others in line: cops, clerks, and people from all professions. As they're talking, they see a man dressed in white, carrying a medical bag, approach the head of the line. He says a couple of words to St. Peter and is immediately ushered into heaven.

The salesman is irate. He wasn't pushed around in life, and he isn't about to start getting pushed around now. He makes his way to the head of the line and lets St. Peter have it. "I've been waiting here for hours, and some clown who thinks he's something special 'cause he's got on a white coat elbows his way into Heaven in front of all of the rest of us. What gives?"

"Calm down, fella, don't get so upset," soothed St. Peter. "That was just God playing doctor."

•

What do you get when you cross a prostitute with a computer salesman?

A fucking know-it-all.

Little Jason came up to his father at the breakfast table one morning and declared, "Daddy, when I grow up, I want to be just like you."

"Aw, son, that makes me feel great," said his Dad, patting him on the head. "I'd love to have a salesman for a son."

"That's not what I mean, Daddy," said Jason. "I mean I want to fuck Mommy."

•

By the time Cuozzi pulled into the little town, every hotel room was taken. "You've got to have a room somewhere," he pleaded. "Or just a bed —I don't care where."

"Well, I do have a double room with one occupant," admitted the manager, "and he might be glad to split the cost. But to tell you the truth, he snores so loudly that people in adjoining rooms have complained in the past. I'm not sure it'd be worth it to you."

"No problem," said the salesman. "I'll take it."

The next morning Cuozzi came down to breakfast bright-eyed and bushy-tailed. "How'd you sleep?" asked the manager.

"Never better."

The manager was impressed. "No problem with your roommate's snoring, then?"

"Nope. I shut him up in no time."

"How'd you manage that?"

"He was already in bed, snoring away, when I came in the room," Cuozzi explained. "I went over, gave him a kiss on the cheek, said, 'Goodnight, darling,' and he sat up all night watching me."

●

Coming on hard times, the company cut its commission rate to the sales force. Hoping to ease the inevitable hard feelings, the sales manager decided to visit a few of the reps' offices the next Monday. "I'm afraid we were a bit late cutting the checks on Friday, Jenny," he said jovially. "Have any trouble getting it cashed?"

"No problem at all, Fred," she replied sarcastically. "I swapped it for a magazine on the way home."

●

The regional sales manager was chewing out one of the sales reps about his report. "For God's sake, Dawson, it's barely legible, and so scrambled I can't make heads or tails of it. A good sales report is a tool for the whole company: any fool should be able to understand it."

"I couldn't agree more," responded Dawson affably. "Which part of the report did you have trouble with?"

•

The CEO of a large pharmaceutical company employed three extremely competent sales-women, and when his sales manager decided to retire, the CEO couldn't pick which one to promote. After racking his brains comparing their respective qualifications, he finally came up with the idea of leaving $1000 in cash on each one's desk and seeing what happened.

Sally returned the envelope first thing the next morning.

Valerie invested the money in the market overnight, made $1500, kept $500, and returned his $1000.

Brenda invested the money overnight, made $1500, and turned over $1500 to him the next day.

So who got the promotion?

The one with the biggest tits!

•

Definition of a promoter: someone who wants to sell you something you don't want that he doesn't have.

•

When Dan's house burned down, his first phone call was to the woman who'd sold him his homeowner's policy. "I need a check for the cash value of my house, and I need it as soon as possible," he instructed.

"I'm afraid it doesn't work that way," explained the insurance agent politely. "See, yours was a replacement policy, which means that we'll be rebuilding the house exactly as it was before."

"I see," said Dan, after a long pause. "In that case, I want to cancel the policy on my wife."

•

Nussbaum the peddler was busted for selling woolen hats without a license, and found himself hauled into court along with three prostitutes who had been arraigned on the same day.

"It's all a case of mistaken identity," protested the first streetwalker to be summoned before the bench. "See, I'm mindin' my own business when this car pulls up—"

"Drop it," interrupted the judge. "I've seen you in this courthouse at least a dozen times before. That'll be a hundred and fifty dollars, and it'll be twice that if I set eyes on you again. Next!"

The second hooker whined, "I was just on my way to secretarial school, Judge, to learn how to make an honest dollar, when—"

"Cut the crap," the magistrate broke in. "Two hundred and fifty bucks or ten days in jail—you choose. Next!"

The third woman came forward and declared, "Your Honor, I plead guilty: I'm a prostitute. It's not the living I'd choose, but it's the only way I can make enough to feed and clothe my family, so it's what I do."

The Judge smiled. "Finally, someone who realizes a courtroom is a place to tell the truth. To reward your honesty, young woman, I'm dismissing your case. In fact, Mr. O'Brien"—he turned and summoned the bailiff—"make sure Miss Cardoza gets seventy-five dollars from the Policemen's Benevolent Fund. Next?"

Up stepped Nussbaum the peddler, who had been paying close attention. "Your Honor," he said frankly, "I'm not gonna lie to you either. I'm a prostitute."

•

What's the difference between a woman who sells used cars and a barracuda?

Nail polish.

•

Two WASPy brokers were walking down the street. One turned to the other and said, "You know, you're my best friend, but you never ask: 'How're you doing? How're sales? How's business?'"

"Okay," responded his friend. "How're sales?"

"Oh, fine."

•

The real-estate agent sized up the newly-married young couple as the only possible buyers for a listing she'd carried for over a year. Showing them around, she extolled the house's meager charms, racking her brain for everything positive she could conceivably imagine. To her delight, the couple seemed to like the place, and were inquiring about financing when something crashed through the living room window, shattering it into smithereens.

"What the hell was that?" demanded the husband, as his wife dove for cover.

"Another plus," cried the realtor brightly. "You're only a stone's throw from the public school!"

•

After only a few weeks on the job, the sales associate was given the key to the executive washroom. "Gee, Mr. Phillipson, this is really a privilege. I'll be honored to use it," he stammered happily.

"I know you will, Ralph," his boss assured him. "And just be sure it's neat and clean at the end of the day."

•

The sales rep's wife got a postcard while he was on the road. What did it say?

"Having a great time. Wish you were her."

•

A saleswoman assigned to a new territory got hopelessly lost looking for an obscure depot in the Midwest. Finally she pulled up to a tiny farmhouse, where barking dogs brought the farmer into the yard. "How can I help you?" he asked amiably.

"Ever hear of Ellerton? Can you give me directions?"

The farmer scratched his head for what seemed like minutes, then replied. "Nope, can't say that I have."

"Thanks anyway," said the rep politely. She reversed the car, backed down the drive to the gate, got out, opened the gate, drove through, stopped again, closed the gate, and had just started up again when she heard a faint yell. Looking in the rearview mirror, she spotted the farmer beckoning her urgently. So she opened the gate again, drove through, latched it again, drove back up to the farmhouse, and pulled up next to the waving man.

"Just thought I'd let you know," the beaming farmer explained. "I went in and asked the wife, and she doesn't know the way to Ellerton, either."

•

The recent high-school graduate applied for a position as sales rep with a bottled-water company, and proudly handed over all her papers.

The personnel director looked them over carefully, then looked up at the applicant. "These lifesaving certificates certainly are impressive, Miss Lansing," she commented graciously, "but frankly we were hoping you could *sell* our product, not swim in it."

•

Levin, a notoriously tightfisted sales analyst, alleviated his few twinges of conscience by giving a quarter to the miserable-looking woman who sold bagels from a pushcart on the corner by his office. He never bought a bagel, having already breakfasted, but he always put a coin into her grimy palm and felt himself a virtuous man.

This went on for months, until one day the bagel-seller tugged at his immaculate cuff. "Mister, Mister, I gotta tell ya somethin'."

"Ah," acknowledged Levin with a gracious smile, "I suppose you wish to know why I give you a quarter every day but never take the bagel?"

"Nah, that's yer business," she snorted. "My business is tellin' ya the price's gone up to thirty-five cents."

•

The fellow made an appointment with the town banker and explained with great excitement that he'd come across a formula which would make pussy smell like an orange. "All I need's a little cash to start up with."

The banker listened politely but turned down the loan, remarking that it just didn't sound to him like a sound business proposition. A year or so later, though, he noticed that the man's bank account had swelled to impressive proportions, so the banker invited him back for a second meeting. "Say, I hope there are no hard feelings about my turning down that loan last year," he began rather apologetically.

"Nope, none at all," replied the entrepreneur cheerfully. "In fact, quite the opposite. See, you got me to thinking, and I figured you had a point. So I went to work on a formula to make an orange taste like pussy—and it's selling like crazy."

•

A Jewish sales agent was hired by an insurance company and did exceptionally well for them, so well that the directors all agreed that he should be made a director himself. There was a problem, however: all the directors were devout Catholics, and the firm's bylaws stipulated that this remain the case. Finally, Gilligan came up with a solution. "We'll just call in Father O'Shea to convert him."

So a meeting was set up between Father O'Shea and Mr. Feingold, and the two men were alone in the office for a good two hours. When the door finally opened, Gilligan pulled Father O'Shea aside and asked if he'd succeeded in converting the agent.

The priest shook his head. "No, but he did sell me a hundred and seventy-five thousand dollars' worth of life insurance."

•

The proprietor of a small computer-hardware company called his three-person sales force into his office for a staff meeting. "Fellas," he announced brightly, "we're having a terrific spring sales contest this year. The salesman who sells the most units by the end of April gets a week-long Carnival Caribbean cruise. The runner-up gets a set of steak knives. Third place wins a permanent vacation with no pay."

•

A year later the same company was on the edge of bankruptcy. The owner summoned his two-man sales force into his office. "Things aren't going too well, guys," he announced grimly, "so to perk up sales I'm announcing another contest. This time the winner gets a blow job . . . and the loser gets to give it."

The stockbroker received notice from the IRS that he was being audited. He showed up at the appointed time and place with all his financial records, then sat for what seemed like hours as the accountant pored over them. Finally the IRS agent looked up and commented, "You must have been a tremendous fan of Sir Arthur Conan Doyle."

"Why would you say that?" wondered the broker.

"Because you've made more brilliant deductions on your last three returns than Sherlock Holmes made in his entire career."

•

Though ventriloquism was his secret passion, Fernandez had made a lot of money in real estate, and he decided to retire as a gentleman farmer. He found a place he liked, but felt it was somewhat overpriced. So he decided to put both of his skills to work and have some fun with the farmer as they toured the outbuildings.

"How's the barn holding up?" he asked, turning towards the swaybacked horse in a corner stall.

"The roof leaks, and the tractor's thirty-five years old," replied the horse. The farmer, not realizing it was Fernandez throwing his voice, turned pale.

"Mooo," said the cow in answer to the ventriloquist's next question. "My stall's falling apart and the feed's all moldy."

The farmer started to quake.

Next were the chickens. "Need a new coop, holes in the wire," they cackled.

"Just a dang minute," interrupted the farmer, grabbing his prospective buyer by the shoulders. "Don't talk to the sheep—they lie."

•

The owner of a well-established firm of wholesalers was interviewing people for a position in sales. One candidate offered excellent references and experience, and was well-dressed and well-spoken. The only catch was a disconcerting mannerism: the fellow couldn't seem to stop winking.

So the sales manager decided to be frank. "You've got all the qualifications for the job and I'd really like to hire you—but I'm afraid that facial tic of yours might put customers off."

"I'm glad you brought that up, sir," said the sales candidate, "because all I need to make that annoying wink go away is a couple of aspirin. See for yourself, I've got some on me." And he began emptying his pockets on the desk.

The prospective employer was startled to see

dozens of packages of condoms piling up: ribbed ones, lubricated ones, multicolored ones, every variety imaginable.

"Aha," cried the young man happily, "here they are." He brandished two aspirin, swallowed them, and sure enough, the tic went away in less than a minute.

"So much for the wink," said the sales manager sternly, gesturing at the mountain of rubbers, "but what about all this stuff here? I don't want my company to be represented by some wild womanizer, after all."

"No fear. I'm a happily married man."

"So how can you account for the contents of your pockets?"

"It's simple, sir. Did you ever go into a drug store, winking like crazy, and ask for a packet of aspirins?"

•

The retired sales manager of a chain of discount stores was reading the paper early one morning when the phone rang. It was Father MacRae, an old friend, pleading for his help. "At eleven I have to officiate at a funeral on the other side of the county," explained the agitated priest, "and at the same time I'm supposed to be hearing confessions. Richie, could you cover the confessions for me?"

Shocked, the ex-discounter protested that he

lacked the training and experience, but the priest assured him there wasn't really all that much to it. "Come on down after the eight-thirty mass and listen to what I say to the parishioners —you'll get the hang of it."

So Richie reluctantly agreed, and was in the confessional with Father MacRae when a young woman entered the other side and said, "Forgive me Father, for I have sinned."

"What have you done, my child?" asked the priest gently.

"I have had impure thoughts," she admitted softly, "and then I had sex with my boyfriend."

"How many times?" asked the priest.

"Four times," admitted the girl.

"Say twenty 'Hail Marys', put twenty dollars in the collection plate, and the Lord will forgive you," he assured her.

The next person to enter the confessional was a woman who admitted to having had sexual relations with a married man.

"How many times?" asked Father MacRae gravely.

"Twice this week."

"For your penance, say ten 'Our Fathers' and put ten dollars in the collection plate," Father MacRae told her. Then he turned to Richie and whispered, "Got the hang of it?"

Richie said he thought he could handle it, and the priest raced off to the funeral. The next woman entered the confessional and said, "Forgive me, Father, for I have sinned. I have had sex out of wedlock."

"I see," murmured the ex-salesman solemnly. "How many times?"

"Just once, Father."

"Well, you better get out and do it again," Richie advised.

"Do it again?!" The woman was shocked.

"Why not? This week it's two for ten bucks!"

●

Goldfarb the knitwear king received word that one of his top salespeople had succumbed to a heart attack while in the field. In response, he cabled, "RETURN SAMPLES VIA UPS AND SEARCH POCKETS FOR ORDERS."

●

"My daughter Lauren thinks money grows on trees," the overworked divisional sales manager complained to his secretary one day. "Tonight she's getting a talking-to that'll really get across the value of a dollar."

The next morning, the secretary asked, "How'd it go?"

"Not so good," the manager admitted glumly. "Now the kid wants her allowance in Deutschmarks."

What's the difference between a securities salesman and a pair of jockey shorts?

A pair of jockey shorts only has to cover one
asshole at a time.

•

A man walked into a fancy dress store and announced to the owner, "I'm the greatest salesperson ever. And I want a job."

"That's quite a claim," the owner responded,
"but unfortunately I don't have any openings."

Undaunted, the salesperson asked, "How
many dresses does your best employee sell in a
day?"

"Five or six," the owner answered.

Without blinking an eye, the fellow claimed,
"I'll sell twelve and I'll do it without pay or commission."

The owner, knowing she couldn't lose, agreed.
And, indeed, just an hour before closing, the
new salesperson had sold eighteen dresses. "Do
I get the job now?" he asked.

"I've got one more test for you," the owner
declared. She went back into the storeroom and
came back out with the most hideous dress
imaginable. "Sell this dress by the time the store
closes tonight and you've got a job."

Forty-five minutes later, the guy marched into her office and threw down the sales receipt.

"I'm impressed," the owner admitted in amazement. "You've got the job. How on earth did you convince somebody to buy that thing?"

"Getting the woman to buy it wasn't a problem. The hard part was strangling her seeing-eye dog."

•

The sales manager was exhorting her crew of door-to-door salesmen to greater efforts. "Here's a line that always works," she suggested. "Hold up the product and say, 'Now here's one that your neighbors were sure you couldn't afford.'"

•

"Good news," announced the head of the company when the sales manager showed up for his appointment. "We've discovered how to increase sales dramatically."

"That's wonderful, sir. What can I do to help?" she asked eagerly.

"Quit."

One night Fred came home from work and told his wife over dinner that he had just signed up with the company hockey team. Worried that he might hurt himself, his wife went out the next day to buy him a jock strap.

The effeminate sales clerk was only too happy to help her. "They come in colors, you know," he told her. "We have Virginal White, Ravishing Red, and Promiscuous Purple."

"I guess white will do just fine," she said.

"They come in different sizes, too, you know," said the clerk.

"Gee, I'm really not sure what Fred's size is," confessed his wife. So the clerk extended his pinkie.

"No, it's bigger than that."

The clerk extended a second finger.

"No, it's bigger than that," said the wife.

A third finger.

"Still bigger," she said.

When the clerk stuck out his thumb, too, she said, "Yes, that's about right."

So the clerk put all five fingers in his mouth, pulled them out, and pronounced expertly, "That's a medium."

The persistent sales rep pounced on the firm's head buyer as he headed out the door to lunch. "If I could just have a few moments of your time this afternoon, Mr. Lewis," he began.

The executive brushed him off. "I'm in a hurry. Just make a date with my secretary, all right?"

"Sir, I've made several dates with your secretary," the salesman informed him, "and she's a great lay, but I still want to see *you.*"

•

Did you hear about the enterprising salesperson who sold three boxcars of Venetian blinds to the Somalis?

She pointed out they could use them for bunk beds.

•

The livestock dealer paid a visit to a local dairy farmer and expressed his interest in buying a cow. The farmer pointed out a good-looking animal, assured him that she gave plenty of milk and had a good disposition, and they settled on a price of $175.

But as the dealer was loading her into his truck, he noticed that the beast was blind. He turned furiously on the farmer. "How the hell do you expect me to sell a cow that's blind?" he roared.

The farmer shrugged. *"I* just did."

•

A Pole is walking down the street and passes a hardware store advertising a sale on a chainsaw capable of cutting 700 trees in seven hours. The Pole thinks that's a great deal and decides to buy one.

The next day, he comes back with the saw and complains to the salesman that the thing didn't come close to chopping down the 700 trees the ad said it would.

"Let's test it out back," offers the salesman. Finding a log, the salesman pulls the starter cord and the saw makes a great roaring sound.

"Jeepers!" exclaims the Pole. "What's that noise?"

•

Asking for directions in the Ozarks is often a chancy business, and the desperate rep finally pulled up to a little shanty to ask directions to Culbertville. The toothless redneck on the porch said, "Take this here road past where it bottoms out in the creek next to the billboard for Willamette's Feed and Grain. Turn right just after that onto Hitch's Lane—there ain't no sign—for about four miles, 'til you come to the dam. Hang a left, follow along by the pond 'til you come to this big pine tree overhanging the gully, turn left again, and go 'bout three more miles."

"And that'll get me to Culbertville?" asked the rep, scribbling furiously.

"Nope, it'll get you back here. If'n I gave you all the directions, you'd jest git confused."

●

"There's no doubt about it, sir, this car is the opportunity of a lifetime," enthused the salesman at Joe's Previously Owned Automobile Emporium.

"No doubt," agreed the prospective customer dubiously. "I can hear it knocking."

●

"Don't let me pressure you, Mrs. Schmidt," said the aggressive life-insurance salesman. "Why don't you sleep on my offer and call me in the morning? Assuming you wake up."

Eager to make her mark in the world of sales and marketing, the attractive new MBA took a job as executive assistant to the middle-aged sales manager of a fast-growing computer software company. She found the work challenging and the travel interesting, but was extremely annoyed by her boss's tendency to treat her in public as though she were his girlfriend rather than a professional associate.

This was especially irritating in restaurants, where he would insist on ordering for her, and on calling her "dearest" or "darling" within earshot of the waiters. When she told him how much it bothered her, he promised to stop, but the patronizing behavior continued. Finally, as he led her into a four-star restaurant, she took matters into her own hands.

"Where would you like to sit, sweetheart?" he asked, with a wink at the maitre d'.

"Gee," she replied, "anywhere you say, Daddy."

•

When a hooker set up business in a trailer next to the town's bottling plant, the all-male sales department swiftly lined up outside her door. The hooker looked over the gathering and made it clear she wanted to move things right along. "Unbuckle your belts and get out your wallets," she instructed. "You get ten minutes for twenty bucks."

Well, the first customer was so excited that he shot his wad in just a few minutes. But the timer went off when the second guy was still pumping away. When the woman started to get up, he angrily pointed out that he hadn't come yet.

"Too bad, buddy," said the hooker. "I've got a business to run. You'll just have to come back."

"Listen, lady," he said, "all those guys out there work for the bottling plant. And you know what the company motto is?"

She shook her head.

"No deposit, no return."

•

A cable television station featured an interview with America's Salesperson of the Year. After the usual questions about where the honoree had grown up and what had drawn her to a career in sales, the interviewer said bluntly, "So, Salesperson of the Year, sell me something, right now."

"What would you like me to sell you?" she asked, unruffled.

Looking around the set, the interviewer settled on a vase of dried flowers on a corner table. "How about that vase?"

"Fine. What do you want it for?"

"Well, it's kind of pretty, and the colors match my couch, and I can put flowers in it."

"What do you figure it's worth?" asked the salesperson.

"Oh, fifteen bucks, maybe."

"It's yours."

•

What's the best thing about turning sixty-five?

No more calls from insurance salesmen.

•

The Singers went over to the local Oldsmobile dealership to pick out a new car. No sooner had gorgeous Mrs. Singer set foot on the car lot than the salesman's jaw dropped. He couldn't take his eyes off her.

Never one to pass up a chance at a bargain, Singer pulled the salesman aside. "She's really something, eh?" he commented with a sly smile.

The salesman nodded dumbly, eyes glued to Mrs. Singer's cleavage.

"Tell you what," Singer proposed. "You've got a back room here, right? Let's take her back there, and if you can do everything I can do, I'll pay double for that convertible in the corner of the lot. If not, I get it for free."

The salesman agreed enthusiastically, his gaze dropping to Mrs. Singer's perfect, miniskirted ass. As soon as the door was closed, Singer pulled up his wife's t-shirt and started fondling the luscious melons that popped out. The salesman followed suit energetically.

Next Singer circled her navel with his tongue. The salesman licked her whole stomach, trying not to drool.

Next Singer pulled up her teeny-weeny skirt, feeling the soft down of her inner thighs. The salesman followed, the slight tang of Mrs. Singer's pussy almost driving him insane.

Next Singer pulled out his pecker and folded it in half.

The salesman sighed. "What color car d'you want?"

•

What's it called when a broker buys and sells stocks while making love to his wife?

Inside her trading.

•

The bathroom scale manufacturer was very proud of the new model being introduced at the trade fair. "Listen to these features: it's calibrated to a hundredth of a pound; it can measure your height as well, in feet or meters; it gives you a readout via an LED or human-voice simulator; and that's not all—"

"Very impressive," interrupted a none-too-slender sales rep for a chain of home-furnishings stores, "but before I place an order I'll have to try it out."

"Be my guest," said the manufacturer graciously.

But no sooner had the fellow taken his place on the scale than a loud, very human-sounding voice issued forth: "One at a time, please, one at a time!"

•

Why should you be especially nice to female sales executives?

You never know when they'll have an opening you could fill.

•

Then there was the coal salesman who got into an argument with the rep for a home-heating-oil concern. "How can you come right out and claim that your product's better?" he demanded.

"Simple," replied the coal salesman. "Our product goes to the buyer *and* to the cellar!"

•

A woman walked into a lingerie shop in Washington D.C. and said she needed to buy a bra. "Certainly, Miss," said the salesperson. "We stock three kinds: a Democratic bra, a Republican bra, and a Liberal bra. I'm sure one will suit your needs."

"I never heard of those kinds," said the confused customer. "What's the difference?"

The sales clerk explained, "The Democratic bra supports the fallen and uplifts the masses. The Republican bra makes mountains out of molehills. And if you buy a Liberal bra, your cups runneth over."

•

Did you hear about the business started by the Polish salesman?

A self-service massage parlor.

•

Tom started out as a door-to-door salesman, and through much hard work became enormously successful—so much so that he barely had any private life at all. One night his wife said with a sigh, "I wish you wouldn't think about sales and profits and business all the time, Tom."

"I don't think about business all the time," he protested. "What makes you say that?"

"Well, when the woman sitting next to you at the restaurant last night asked if you had a family, you told her you had a wife and two wholly-owned subsidiaries."

●

The ambitious salesperson left a position as a salaried rep to go out on her own. "How's it going, Charlotte?" asked an ex-colleague over lunch a few months later.

"Not as well as I'd hoped," she admitted. "To tell you the truth, I never knew how stupid bosses could be until I started working for myself."

●

When Bruce walked into the pharmacy and asked for rubbers, the girl behind the counter asked politely, "What size, please?"

"Gosh, I don't know," answered Bruce, a little flustered, so she instructed him to use the fence out back to determine the correct size. And as he walked out the back door, she ran out a side door and behind the fence.

The fence had three holes in it.

Putting his penis in the first hole, Bruce felt capable hands gently stroking it. Reluctantly, he pulled it out and inserted it in the second hole, and within seconds, he felt a warm, wet pussy at work on the other side of the fence. Groaning with pleasure, he managed to pull out and stick it through the third hole. There he felt an expert set of lips and tongue give him the blow job of his dreams. Jumping up, the salesgirl hurried back behind the counter and was standing there smiling when Bruce staggered back through the door.

"Your size, sir?" she asked politely.

"Forget the rubbers," he grunted. "Just gimme three yards of that fence."

•

How can you spot the top-billing salesman for a Somali company?

He's the one with a Rolex around his waist.

•

Returning to the office after his first sales trip for Acme, Inc., the sales rep headed for the accounts department to be reimbursed for his expenses. When the clerk handed him the appropriate forms, the rep read them over and shook his head mournfully. "Okay, I'll follow the instructions, but my boss isn't gonna like it one bit, I'll tell you that."

"What're you talking about?" demanded the clerk.

"Just look what it says, right here in the first paragraph," the rep pointed out. " 'Employee must submit a completed expense voucher with all relevant receipts stapled to his department head.' "

•

When the traveling salesman got the message at the hotel desk that his wife had given birth, he rushed to the phone. "Hi honey," he cried happily. "Is it a boy or a girl?"

"Irving, Irving," sighed his wife wearily, "is that all you can think about? Sex, sex, sex?"

•

Two intensely competitive brothers, Bernie and Ernie, both went into sales, and their lives were ruled by the desire to one-up the other. When Bernie got a raise, Ernie was the first to hear about it; when Ernie was promoted to regional sales manager, Bernie was the first person he bragged to; when Bernie got a BMW, Ernie got a Mercedes; when Ernie bought a ski cabin, Bernie bought a yacht; and so on.

When Ernie saw an ad for the very first cellular car phones, he decided to beat his brother to the punch for sure. He was in line when the store opened, waited while the phone was installed, got behind the wheel, and instantly dialed his brother. "Hey there, Bernie," he said breezily, "just thought I'd give you a ring from my new cellular car phone with two speakers, a sixty-number memory, remote—"

"Can you hold on just a minute?" interrupted Bernie. "I'm in the Saab, and the other phone is ringing."

•

What manufacturer leads in vibrator sales?
   Genital Electric.

•

One afternoon the red phone on Prime Minister Major's desk rang.

President Yeltsin was on the line, asking an urgent favor. "The AIDS virus has reached our country and we are suffering from an acute condom shortage. In fact," the President confessed, "there are none at all to be had in the Moscow pharmacies. Would it be possible for you to ship me 850,000 condoms—immediately—so that we can deal with this public health threat?"

"Why certainly, Boris," replied Mr. Major gracefully. "Will Friday do?"

"That would be wonderful," sighed the Russian in evident relief. "Oh, and John, one specification: they must be five inches around and nine inches long."

"No problem at all," the Prime Minister assured him breezily. Hanging up, he had his secretary get the largest condom manufacturer in Great Britain on the line, who informed him that a rush order to those specifications would be no problem for his assembly line. "Excellent, excellent," chirped Major. "Now just two more things . . ."

"Yes, sir?"

"On the condoms must be printed, 'MADE IN GREAT BRITAIN,' " Major instructed.

"But of course," the businessman assured him.

"And 'MEDIUM.' "

•

Sales Manager: "Why do you always deliver your paycheck to the bank by hand?"

Sales Rep: "Because it's too small to go by itself."

•

Tarzan and Jane were expecting their fourth kid and were pretty strapped for cash, so Tarzan decided to go into the used-crocodile business. Monday morning he got up early, shaved, put on a suit, swung down to the riverbank, and spent the whole day fighting, haggling over, and hassling with cranky crocs.

As dusk fell, a wan Tarzan swung back to the treehouse and demanded, "Quick Jane, a martini!" Tossing it back, he barked, "Another, Jane, on the double!" Gulping it down, he held out his glass again. "One more, Jane."

"Aw, honey, don't you think you're overdoing it a bit?" she chided gently.

"You don't understand, Jane—it's a *jungle* out there."

•

What's the sexiest four-letter word to a salesman?

C-A-S-H.

A well-endowed woman entered a chic Madison Avenue boutique and tried on every evening gown in the store. Finally setting eyes on a very sexy, low-cut dress hanging in the display window, she asked the exhausted sales clerk if she could try it on.

"Of course, madam," he muttered through clenched teeth, squeezed into the window, and began the painstaking task of taking the dummy apart to remove the gown. Eventually he succeeded and was able to hand it over to the demanding customer.

"How do I look?" she asked, emerging from the dressing room. "Does it show off my superb breasts to advantage?"

"Oh, absolutely," the clerk assured her, "but do hairy chests run in your family?"

•

Then there was the mom who decided it was time for her son to learn the great American sport of baseball, so off they went to the sporting-goods store. "How much is this baseball glove?" she asked the salesman.

"Twenty dollars."

"And the bat?"

"Ten dollars."

"I'll take the bat."

"Would you like a ball for the bat?" asked the salesman hopefully.

"No," answered the mother after thinking it over for a moment, "but I'll blow you for the glove."

•

What's so depressing about selling hearing aids door-to-door?

Your best prospects never answer.

•

Every year Abramowitz took his sales force out to lunch, and each year the event led off with a brief inspirational speech. This year, Abramowitz got to his feet and began, "In the garment business, there are hundreds of ways to make a fortune, but only one honest way."

"And what's that?" asked a salesman.

Abramowitz shrugged. "How should I know?"

The salesman at Vinnie's Fine Used Cars was dumbfounded when a gorilla came in and asked to see what was available in four-door sedans with standard transmissions. He couldn't think of any reason not to oblige the beast, especially since a huge wad of cash was visibly clutched in its enormous hairy paw, so he showed it all around the lot.

The animal looked under the hoods, checked the odometers for mileage and the bodies for rust, and finally made up its mind. "How much?" asked the gorilla, then handed over the amount in cash.

Finally the car salesman couldn't take it anymore. "You know," he offered, "we don't get too many *gorillas* in here."

And the gorilla returned, "At eighty-six hundred bucks for a 1981 Plymouth, I'm not surprised."

•

"Don't you know you can't sell insurance without a license?" said the lawyer grimly.

The woman shook her head. "I knew I wasn't selling any, but I didn't know the reason."

•

Why was the sales rep so disappointed?

She went to bed with the sales manager, but she only got a small raise.

·

The chicken that the butcher held out was a nice-looking bird, the woman conceded, but would it feed all her dinner guests? Laura shook her head doubtfully. "Do you have a slightly larger one?" she asked.

"Sure thing, lady," replied the butcher cheerfully, heading for the walk-in refrigerator at the back of the shop. In fact he was completely sold out of chickens that day, so he simply plumped up the one in his hands, pulling at it this way and that until it looked a little more substantial. "How's this one?" he asked, displaying it to the customer confidently.

"Very nice," Laura replied happily. "In fact, on second thought, I'll take both."

·

Why did God invent WASPs?

Somebody has to buy retail.

·

"Wish me good luck," said the salesman to his secretary as he headed out the door. "I'm pitching the big Dodgson account today."

A few hours later he slunk back into the office. "What's the matter?" asked his secretary. "Didn't you get an order?"

"Yeah, as a matter of fact I got three of 'em," he replied glumly. "Get your coat, get out, and don't come back!"

•

"I do happen to need somebody," admitted the owner of the hardware store to the unimpressive-looking man who was interested in a job. "But tell me, can you sell?"

"Of course," was the confident reply.

"I mean really *sell*," reiterated the shopkeeper.

"You bet," said the young man.

"I'll show you what I mean," said the owner, going over to a customer who had just walked in and asked for grass seed. "We're having a very special sale on lawn mowers," he told the customer. "Could I interest you in one?"

"What do I need a lawn mower for?" protested the customer. "I don't even have any grass yet."

"Maybe not," said the owner agreeably, "but all that seed's going to grow like crazy someday and then you'll need a lawn mower in the worst way. And you won't find them on sale in mid-summer, that's for sure."

"I guess you've got a point," admitted the fellow. "Okay, I'll take a lawn mower too."

"Think you can do that?" asked the storekeeper of his new employee after he'd written up the bill. The man nodded.

"Okay, good. Now I have to run to the bank. I'll only be gone for a few minutes, but while I'm gone I want you to sell, sell, sell."

The new guy's first customer was a woman who came over and asked where the tampons were.

"Third aisle over, middle of the second shelf."

When she came to the counter to pay, he leaned over and said, "Hey, you wanna buy a lawn mower? They're on sale."

"Why on earth would I want a lawn mower?" she asked, eyeing him suspiciously.

"Well, you aren't going to be screwing," he blurted, "so you might as well mow the lawn."

●

How can you tell when a salesperson's exaggerating?

Her lips are moving.

●

The high point of the annual sales conference for the four veteran salesmen was their Sunday afternoon golf game. They had just teed off on the twelfth hole when an assistant golf pro came tearing across the green, red-faced and out of breath. "Mr. Webster, Mr. Webster," he gasped, "I have terrible news. Your wife has just been killed in a car accident."

Webster turned to his companions, and said, "Guys, I gotta warn you. Six more holes and you're gonna see a man crying his eyes out."

•

A few days after refusing to go to bed with the sales manager, the sales rep stormed into her office. "My commission check's been cut in half!" he yelled.

"That's right," she said sweetly. "Haven't you ever heard of withholding tax?"

•

The salesman checked into his usual hotel, but nothing else about his behavior was typical: he took the cheapest single room, ignored the receptionist's suggestion that he take her out to a show when she got off duty, ordered the dinner special instead of chateaubriand, and had nothing to drink but water.

"What's got into you, Tim?" asked the hotel manager when he was checking out.

"It's what got into my car back at the office," Tim explained unhappily. "My boss."

•

It seems there was this woman who hated wearing underwear. One day she decided to go shopping for a new pair of shoes, and since she was wearing a skirt the salesman was enjoying an excellent view. After the third or fourth pair of shoes, the guy couldn't stand it anymore. "Lady," he said, "that's some beautiful sight. I could eat that pussy full of ice cream."

Disgusted, the woman ran out of the store and went home. When her husband got home from work she told him about the incident and asked him to go beat the shit out of the salesman. And when he flatly refused, she wanted to know why.

"Three reasons," said her husband. "Number one: you shouldn't have been out in a skirt with no underpants. Number two: you have enough shoes to last you ten more years. And number three: any son-of-a-bitch who can eat that much ice cream I don't want to mess with in the first place."

"It's that sales rep from Baker & Taylor, Ms. Dellon," said the assistant to his boss. "It's the third time he's phoned today."

"I have to finish writing this up," replied the sales manager. "Put him on hold with the Muzak tape, and if he's still on in ten minutes, put him through."

•

The good-looking salesman fancied himself quite a Lothario. One night he picked up a woman at a singles bar and brought her home. He was shocked when she got up right afterwards and declared, "You may be cute, but you sure are a lousy lover."

"I don't see what makes you such an expert," declared the salesman indignantly, sitting up in bed, "especially after only forty-five seconds."

•

The young broker came into the Wall Street bar one cold night and ordered a double Chivas on the rocks. "What's up, Chilton?" asked Hackley, who worked for the same company. "You look kind of shaken up. Rough day?"

"Frankly, it's what happened after work. Binky wouldn't put out, so I split, and was walking towards a cab when this really pathetic girl came up and begged me for a handout. She couldn't have been more than fifteen, she was skinny as a rail, she only had on a thin little sweater, her teeth were chattering, and she told me she hadn't had a square meal for days."

"That *does* sound depressing," said Hackley sympathetically.

"I'll say," agreed Chilton with feeling. "I almost broke down and cried while I was screwing her."

•

It's quiz time in the parochial school, and Brother Michael offers a dollar prize to the student who can name the greatest man who ever lived.

"Columbus," offers Joey Caputo.

"Pope John Paul II," volunteers Ivan Witaski.

"Saint Francis of Assisi," says Irving Greenberg, an aspiring salesman. "I would've said Moses," he whispers to a classmate, "but business is business."

•

Three traveling salesmen ran out of gas not far from a hospitable farmer's house. He and his eighteen beautiful daughters invited them in out of the rain and said they could spend the night, although the farmer apologized for the fact that there was only one spare bedroom and two salesmen would have to sleep in the barn. The three salesmen gratefully accepted his offer, for there were no towing services available at that time of night.

The next morning, as they drove away in the car after getting a gallon of gas, the salesmen began to compare notes about the evening's experience. "All I thought about was straw," said the first guy, "because I had to sleep with the horses."

"You think that's bad," piped up the second guy. "All I dreamed about was mud, because I was down there with the pigs. How 'bout you, Phil?"

"I'll tell ya," said Phil blearily, "all I could think about was golf."

"Why golf?" asked the driver.

"Hey, if you shot eighteen holes in one night, that's all you'd be able to think about, either."

•

An ambitious new overseas sales manager for Budweiser beer traveled all the way to Rome and managed to finagle an audience with the

Pope himself. As soon as the two were alone together, he leaned over and whispered, "Your Holiness, I have an offer I think might interest you. I'm in a position to give you a million dollars if you'll change the wording in the Lord's Prayer to 'our daily beer.' Now whaddaya say?"

"Absolutely not," said the shocked Pontiff.

"Hey, I understand; it's a big decision," sympathized the salesman. "How about five million dollars?"

"I couldn't think of it," sputtered the Pope.

"I know it's a tough one. Tell you what—I can go up to fifty million dollars," proposed the salesman.

Asking him to leave the room, the Pope called in the Cardinal and whispered, "When does our contract with Pillsbury expire?"

•

What kind of stocks do brokers sell to Mafiosi?
    Under-the-counter stocks.

•

Henderson, a none-too-bright sales rep, worked in an office where the boss left each day at 11:00 A.M. and was gone for two hours. This became such a regular occurrence that the rest of the sales force decided to spend the two hours in the bar across the street, but Henderson decided to head home for some extra nookie with his wife. When he arrived home, he found his boss busy banging his wife in the bedroom! Well, he walked right out and headed back to the office.

The following day Henderson was working his ass off when everyone headed across to the bar. "Hey, aren't you coming?" asked one of them.

"Hell no," said Henderson, shaking his head vehemently. "I almost got caught yesterday."

•

How can you tell the sales rep who ought to be retired?

He's got White-Out all over his computer screen.

•

The construction-business mogul was delighted when one of his major suppliers sent around a gorgeous new saleswoman, and proceeded to turn all of his charms upon her. Within a few weeks, however, he grew extremely displeased when she didn't obey his every summons for a "sales call". "Listen, baby," he growled one morning, "I happen to be your *numero uno* account. Who gave you the bad advice that you don't gotta show up and put out if I so much as snap my fingers?"

The saleswoman replied sweetly, "My lawyer."

•

Reduced to selling neckties from a portable sidewalk display, Russo thought up a new gimmick. He printed up a sign which read in big letters, ONLY TWENTY MINUTES AT THIS LOCATION.

•

An anthropologist had been studying an obscure Thai hill tribe when he contracted a particularly virulent case of jungle rot and was dead in a week. His heartbroken widow accompanied the casket back to Milwaukee, where she invited his three best friends to attend an intimate funeral. When the brief service was over, she asked each of the friends to place an offering in the casket, as had been the custom of the tribe he had been living with. "It would mean a great deal to Herbie," she said, then broke down into racking sobs.

Moved to tears himself, the first friend, a doctor, gently deposited $100 in the coffin.

Dabbing his cheeks, the second friend, a lawyer, laid $150 on the deceased Herbie's pillow.

The third friend, a salesman, wrote a check for $450, put it in the casket, and pocketed the cash.

•

The new salesman was invited in for a chat with his new boss and told he was going to be sent to Green Bay.

"Green Bay!" blurted the new man. "Only hookers and football players come from Green Bay!"

"Green Bay happens to be my wife's hometown," said the sales manager icily.

"No kidding?" said the salesman, recovering fast. "What position does she play?"

•

Why was the salesman reluctant to take on the sperm bank account?

He realized business would only come in spurts.

•

A woman went to apply for a job as a salesperson for a company that made farming equipment. Not too keen on the idea, the personnel manager for the company pointed out that the territory was huge, and the customers a hard-nosed, cranky, weatherbeaten bunch. "You have to be pretty tough to cut it out here," he warned.

"I'm tough, I really am," she assured him.

"Well, do you drink and smoke?"

"Yes, of course."

"Do you cuss a lot?" asked the interviewer.

"You bet," said the woman. "I cuss like a lumberjack."

"So have you ever been picked up by the fuzz?"

"Well, no," she admitted, "but I've been swung around by the tits a couple of times."

•

Hear about the new movie called *Altered Suits*?

It's about a Jewish salesman who takes acid and buys retail.

•

When the brash young sales associate arrived at La Coupole for his lunch appointment, he spotted Donald Trump at a corner table and went right over. "Excuse me for interrupting your meal, Mr. Trump," he began, "but I know how much you appreciate enterprise and initiative. I'm trying to win over a very important account today—it could really make or break my company—and the clients I'm meeting with would be incredibly impressed if you stopped by our table at some point and said, 'Hello, Mike.' It would be an incredible favor, Mr. Trump, and someday I'll make it up to you, I swear I will."

"Okay, okay," sighed Trump magnanimously, and went back to his smoked pheasant. He finished and was putting on his coat when he remembered the young man's request. Obligingly he went over to his table, tapped him on the shoulder, and said, "Hi, Mike."

"Not now, Don," snapped the young man. "Can't you see I'm eating?"

•

The owner of the dress shop was favorably impressed with an applicant for a sales clerk position with lots of experience, but wanted to know why the applicant had left her previous position.

"I had a problem with a particularly difficult customer," the woman admitted ruefully. "She tried on every single gown in the entire shop, criticized every single one, and then asked me if I didn't think she'd look better in something flowing. I agreed."

The interviewer was puzzled. "What's so objectionable about that?"

"I suggested the river."

•

Why is buying a car from a sleazy used-car dealer like visiting a whorehouse?

You're 100% certain you're gonna get screwed.

•

The international trade fair was in Buffalo this year, and the delegate from Tanzania could only find a room in a second-rate hotel with a communal toilet at the end of the hall. American food played havoc with his insides, and in the middle of the night he dashed for the bathroom, only to find it occupied. In desperation, the poor man rushed back to his room and relieved himself in a paper bag. Then, after looking about the room unhappily, he decided to get rid of the bag in the air shaft outside his window. However, just as he swung his arm back for the toss, the bottom of the bag gave way, and the unfortunate fellow ended up with its contents splattered over the floor, the wall, and part of the ceiling.

Embarrassed and upset, the Tanzanian sought out the night porter, brought him up to his room, and offered him $30 to clean up the mess.

The porter whistled in amazement. "Man, I'd give fifty just to find out what position you were in!"

•

Where can you find the head saleswoman on the trading floor?

On her knees.

•

The newest realtor at the firm was extremely eager to make his first sale. He was handling the phones one day when the caller asked, "Do you sell maternity clothes?"

"I'm afraid not," said the realtor, thinking fast, "but could I interest you in a larger house, perhaps?"

•

After the annual office Christmas party blowout, Martinez woke up with a pounding headache, cotton-mouthed, and utterly unable to recall the events of the preceding evening. After a trip to the bathroom he was able to make his way downstairs, where his wife put some coffee in front of him. "Gigi," he moaned, "tell me what went on last night. Was it as bad as I think?"

"Even worse," she assured the white-faced salesman, voice dripping with scorn. "You made a complete ass of yourself, succeeded in antagonizing the entire board of directors, and insulted the sales manager to his face."

"He's an asshole—piss on him."

"You did," Louise informed him. "And he fired you."

"Well, fuck him," retorted Martinez feebly.

"I did. You're back at work on Monday."

•

What do you call a salesperson with a new car?
  Employed.

•

Moe's bakery did a good business on Sunday mornings, but at 11:30 he closed up in order to attend the noon service. As he walked to church, a woman said politely, "Sir, your business is open."

"It certainly isn't," he snapped, "because I just locked the door." As he came down the aisle, an acquaintance in the back pew shot him a meaningful glance and whispered, "Your business is open." Suddenly Moe realized what they'd been referring to, and dashed out of the church. Swiftly he tracked down the first woman who had addressed him and, blushing fiercely, asked, "Excuse me, Miss, but when you commented on my business . . . was my salesman in or out?"

•

What's the toughest sell in Somalia?
  After-dinner mints.

•

The banker liked to encourage young entrepreneurs, so when a young lad came in to make an eighty-dollar deposit, the banker came over and patted the youth on the shoulder. "You must be a pretty enterprising fellow," he remarked. "How'd you earn the money?"

  "Selling Christmas cards door-to-door," the boy replied.

  "Good for you! You must have sold them to everyone in the neighborhood."

"No sir." The boy shook his head. "One family bought them all—their dog bit me."

•

Over breakfast in the corner diner, the salesman peered out at the snow piling up against the window. "Think the roads are clear enough to make some sales calls?" he mused out loud.

The waiter shrugged. "I guess it depends on whether you're working on salary or commission."

•

The insurance agent thought he'd heard them all, until the line rang with a certain Mr. Schultz on the line. He listened to the man's tale of woe, then said politely, "I'm sorry, Mr. Schultz, but Mrs. Schultz's latest pregnancy is *not* covered by your accident insurance."

•

Two sales managers got into a conversation at a trade exhibition. "You really have a terrific sales force," complemented one. "How do you find such good people?"

"I've developed some special testing techniques," confided the other. "One of them is to send a candidate out looking for an apartment carrying a suitcase and a trombone."

•

Why are gay salesmen so fiscally responsible?
They always want to make ends meet.

•

Marveling at a certain employee's ability to sell toothbrushes, the head of the sales department decided to follow him around one day. He trailed the salesman to a busy street corner, where he proceeded to set up an array of toothbrushes and a small bowl of brownish stuff surrounded by chips. The salesman would then select a likely customer and announce, "Good morning! We're introducing Nifty Chip Dip— would you like a free sample?"

Tasting the dip, the customers would invariably spit it out in disgust and howl, "It tastes like shit!"

"It is," the salesman would calmly inform them. "Care to buy a toothbrush?"

·

Did you hear about the inspired salesperson who sold 10,000 bathtubs to Haiti?

They're being refitted as passenger ferries.

·

The best-selling agent for the insurance company was the fellow who handled the rural territories. At his retirement dinner he finally confessed the secret of his success. "I deal with farmers, see, and farmers are always working. So I always hired a local farmhand and took him along with me. Whatever the farmer was busy with when I drove up, the hired hand would offer to take over. And the farmer, glad to take a break, was always happy to listen to me."

·

When the legendary salesman was pestered for his secrets of success, he gave a humble shrug. "I'm sure you all know the cardinal rules: know your product, make lots of calls, never take no for an answer. But, frankly, I owe my success to consistently missing a three-foot putt by two inches."

Two shoe salespeople were sent to a remote island in the Pacific. One cabled back, "Come and get me. They don't wear shoes here."

The other cabled, "Send more shoes. No one has any."

A persistent salesperson was told that his prospective customer was out of the office, so he simply made himself comfortable in the waiting room. After nearly three hours, the head of the company got tired of being a virtual prisoner in his office, and admitted the salesman.

"My secretary told you several times I was out. How'd you know I was here?" he asked in grudging admiration.

"Nothing to it," said the salesperson breezily. "She was working."

What do you call a Wall Street trader who smokes pot?

A stocktoker.

During the Great Depression, a travelling salesman made a precarious living travelling around the country by train selling folding ironing boards. One evening the upper Pullman berth opposite his was occupied by an attractive woman, and the two got to talking. Pretty soon he invited her to come over and visit with him.

Blushing, the woman declined. "How'm I going to get over there, anyway? I'm in my stocking feet."

"No problem," said the salesman cheerfully. "I've got something good and solid right here with me that I can put across the aisle."

"Well, all right," said the woman, still somewhat doubtful.

"I wouldn't do it, dearie," chirped a little old lady from a lower berth. "How do you think he's going to get you back?"

•

This sales manager dies and arrives at the Pearly Gates at the same time as the Pope. The Pope is assigned to a hovel and given a dry crust of bread, while the sales manager is ushered into a huge mansion where a staff of servants is placed at his disposal. "What's the story?" the Pope angrily demands of St. Peter. "I was the head of the whole Catholic Church and I'm stuck in a dump, and you give this sales manager the run of the place."

"Well, Your Holiness," St. Peter gently explained, "we have literally hundreds of popes here in heaven, but we've never had a sales manager before."

•

"IF YOU DON'T BUY THIS MAGAZINE, WE'LL KILL THIS DOG." Cover of the *National Lampoon,* January 1973

•

Cohen and Weinstein were discussing the affairs of a fellow textile merchant. "Did you hear about Schwartz?" asked Cohen.

"Hear what? How's business for him?"

"Finished. Over the weekend his warehouse burned to the ground."

"Such a nice guy, Schwartz," responded Weinstein. "And finally he gets the good luck he deserves."

•

A nerdy-looking fellow shuffled timidly into the sales manager's office. "I don't suppose you want to buy any life insurance?" he asked hesitantly.

"No, I don't."

"That's what I figured. Well, thanks anyway." And he turned and made gratefully for the door.

"Hang on a sec, young man," the executive called out. "You know, I've worked with salespeople all my life, and I have to say that was the most pathetic sales pitch I've ever encountered. You have to have confidence, my boy. Shoulders back, look the customer in the eye, believe in yourself! In fact, just to give you a little boost, I'll give you a sale right now. Write me up for that policy after all."

"Thank you, sir, ever so much," said the salesman gratefully, presenting him with the papers.

The sales manager signed with a flourish. "And now that you're feeling more confident, you should learn some tricks of the trade."

"Quite right sir, good idea," said the salesman humbly. "Always useful. Actually, the one I just used is for sales managers."

•

Two salesmen were chatting on the commuter train. "So, Barry, after all these years of marriage, how's your sex life?" asked Kevin.

"Terrific," replied Barry smugly.

"I'm impressed—how do you manage that?"

"It's easy," confided the salesman. "First I get on top, and then I pretend I'm negotiating with one of my customers."

•

Why are paper salesman so popular in gay neighborhoods?

Because they're always good for a ream or two.

•

A Chinese immigrant who ran a laundry bought his supplies from an Italian guy. One day he asked him why his prices kept going up.

"The market's fluctuating," was Rizzuto's answer.

Next week Wong was annoyed to note that prices had gone up again.

"The market's still fluctuating," explained Rizzuto.

A week later prices went up yet again. Outraged, Wong turned to Rizzuto and said, "What happened? Flucked again?"

•

"Hello, sonny, is your mom at home?" asked the door-to-door salesman of the boy who opened the door.

"Yes, she is," he replied, and disappeared back inside the house.

After quite a long wait, the salesman rang the bell again. "I thought you said your mother was home," he said when the boy reappeared.

"She is. But this isn't my house."

•

Helen and Wilbur fell in love. But there was a terrible problem, a sobbing Helen confessed to her mother one night in the kitchen. "Wilbur's a strict Baptist, Mom, and he won't even consider marrying a Catholic, even though he loves me with all his heart."

"Aw, honey, don't despair," consoled her mother. "Think of it as an opportunity for some real salesmanship. I bet you'd do a great job convincing Wilbur just how wonderful the Catholic faith really is. Why, we're the first Christian church, after all. What about our martyrs and saints? Think of all the extraordinary good works Catholics have performed, the missionaries the Church has sent to the darkest corners of the earth, the splendid religious art it's inspired —just look at the treasures of the Vatican—the extraordinary cathedrals commemorating our faith all across the civilized world, the thousands of schools and universities staffed by dedicated Catholic teachers. Think of the promise of salvation Catholicism offers, the comfort and inspiration offered by our priests as they listen to our confessions and forgive our sins. You know all this, Helen, honey. Go on out and sell Wilbur on the Church!"

Helen dried her tears, made a date with Wilbur, and promised to give it her best shot. But when she got home, she collapsed in tears in her mother's arms. "What's the matter, sweetie?" cried her mother. "Didn't it work?"

"It worked all right," moaned Helen. "I *oversold* him—he's decided to become a priest."

•

The carnival barker was giving an inspired pitch to the crowds strolling by his sideshow tent one night. "Come one, come all! Behold the most amazing man you'll ever see, a superhero of our times! Only fifty cents to shake the hand of someone who heals the sick, makes the lame walk again, gives sight to the blind and—yes, ladies and gentlemen—even makes the dead come alive!"

"Who're you selling in there?" heckled a skeptical passerby. "Jesus Christ?"

"No sir," replied the barker happily. "Lee Iacocca."

Why is .it easy to become a successful salesperson?

Because humans are the only animals that can be skinned more than once.

•

The farmer had to drive into the city for some equipment, and while he was downtown he decided to buy a present for his wife. Feeling extremely self-conscious, he went into a lingerie shop, where a nice saleswoman asked if he needed any help.

"I sure do," blurted the farmer. "Don't go in for much of this stuff. I want to buy one of those." And he pointed to a bra on a mannequin in the window.

"What a nice choice," said the saleswoman encouragingly. "What size?"

"Jees, I don't know," replied the farmer, blushing.

"Let's see . . . are they like coconuts?" she asked helpfully.

The farmer shook his head vehemently.

"How about grapefruit?"

"Oh, no."

"Oranges, then?" suggested the saleswoman.

"Nope."

"Lemons, perhaps?" she asked tactfully.

The farmer shook his head again, now sweating profusely.

"Well then, eggs maybe?"

"That's it!" cried the farmer in great relief. "Eggs—fried."

•

What's a seasoned salesman's idea of a balanced breakfast?

A drink in each hand.

•

The junior bond salesman seemed to be having a hard time, and finally, after a potential client had stormed out of the guy's office, one of the more experienced men took him aside for a little chat. "You know, Sussberg, he counseled, "tact is a big part of being a successful salesman."

"Of course I know that," blustered the younger guy. "What makes you bring it up?"

"Well, I'm just wondering what you told that really ugly guy who just blasted out of your office. Did he ask you what he should do with his money?"

Sussberg nodded unhappily.

"And what did you recommend?" pressed the senior salesman.

"Plastic surgery," he admitted.

•

The antique-book salesman walked into the whorehouse and said politely, "Madam, may I have the pleasure of making the acquaintance of one of your comely employees for the pursuit of carnal pleasures this evening?"

The madam looked over the nerdy-looking fellow, sizing him up as pretty scrawny, but well-spoken and mannerly. "All my girls are busy," she replied, "but if you'd care to, I'm available."

The book salesman agreed and followed her back to her room. Undressed he was no more impressive, especially since his penis was only three inches long, but when he commanded, "Rise, Caesar, rise!" it grew to a robust eleven inches. And he and the madam proceeded to screw for several hours.

At long last she said with a sigh, "I gotta say, this has been one of the best nights of my professional life. Would you mind if I called in my girls to take a look at you before you leave? You're really something special, you know."

But the modest salesman declined, explaining, "I came to bury Caesar, not to praise him."

•

Why did General Motors set up an employment office in Harlem?

It's the best place in the country to find crack salesmen.

•

A stranger walks into a bar and announces in a loud voice to the bartender, "Hey, have I got some terrific salesman jokes for you!"

The bartender leans over to him and whispers, "Listen, if I were you I'd watch my tongue. See those ten guys sitting over there by the window? They're part of the Xerox sales force." He points down to the end of the bar. "Those guys there sell for Kodak, and that group of six standing around the juke box work in sales for Colgate-Palmolive."

"Oh, that's okay," the stranger responds cheerfully. "I'll talk v-e-r-y s-l-o-w-l-y."

•

Hear about the industrious salesman who made a million dollars in Poland with Cheerios?

He sold them as doughnut seeds.

What did the travelling salesman say to the one-legged hitchhiker?

"Hop in!"

•

A doctor, an architect and a bonds salesman were arguing about who had the smartest dog. They decided to settle the issue by getting all the dogs together and seeing whose could perform the most impressive feat.

"Okay, Corbusier," said the architect, and the dog trotted over to the table and in ten minutes had constructed a full-scale model of Chartres out of toothpicks. Pretty impressive, everyone agreed, and the architect gave Corbusier a cookie.

"Hit it, Kildare," said the doctor, and Kildare lost no time in performing a successful emergency Caesarian section on a cow. Not bad, conceded the other two, and Kildare got a cookie from the doctor.

"Go, Boesky!" ordered the bonds salesman. So Boesky fucked the other two dogs, took the cookies and went out to lunch.

•

A salesman walks into a bar with a briefcase full of frogs and sets it down next to the prettiest girl there. "These are very special frogs," he informs her.

"What's so special about your frogs?" she asks.

He beams, "These frogs are specially trained to eat pussy."

The girl slaps him, knocking him off his chair, and accuses him of telling a filthy lie.

"No, it's true," he assures her as he gets up off the floor. "And to prove it, I'll give you a free demonstration."

After much discussion she agrees, and they go to her apartment. She gets undressed and positions herself appropriately on the bed. He takes one of the frogs out of his briefcase and carefully puts it between her legs. "Okay, Froggie," he commands, "do your stuff!"

Despite the salesman's exhortations, which increase in volume and desperation, the frog just sits there. The girl starts to snicker.

"Okay, buddy," says the salesman, moving the frog out of the way, "I'm only going to show you one more time."

•

How do salesmen say "Fuck you!"?
    "Trust me."

A cocky salesman strutted into a small-town saloon, sidled up to the bar, and told the bartender he'd bet him $50 he could make him cry in three minutes. "You've got a deal!" exclaimed the bartender. "I haven't cried since I broke my leg when I was ten."

So two and a half minutes went by in silence, and finally the bartender pointed out, "You know, you only have thirty seconds left and I'm nowhere near crying."

"No problem," replied the salesman. "My friend Boo will be along any moment, and he'll have you crying in no time."

"Boo who?" asked the bartender . . . and then sheepishly handed over the fifty bucks.

The salesman proceeded down the bar to where an African-American was nursing a beer, and made him the same offer. "Man," shouted the African-American, "ah ain't cried since ah was a baby. You got a deal!"

A minute and a half silently ticked by, and the African-American spoke up, pointing out that time was running out.

"Don't worry," the salesman answered, "my friend Boo is due right about now."

"Who be Boo?" asked the African-American.

It was the first day at IBM for the young sales-person, and she was busy getting her desk in order when another salesperson walked by. "Excuse me, Mr. Frothingham, can you tell me where the Harrison file is at?"

"Young lady," came the reply, "at IBM we do not end our sentences with a preposition."

"All right," said the new person without skipping a beat, "can you tell me where the Harrison file is at, asshole?"

•

A Jewish tire company called Firestein needed a catchy tag line to distinguish it from its main competitor, Firestone. You know what a bright salesman came up with?

"Firestein tires not only stop on a dime—they pick it up!"

•

Hear about the leper who made his living as a salesman?

He did great until business fell off.

•

Two guys were walking across the street when they ran into a mutual friend, and they commented on how prosperous-looking he was. It turned out he had every reason to be: he was head salesman at a major computer hardware company and had just had one of the best years in the history of the company.

"I can't complain," he bragged. "I've got a sixty-foot yacht, a beautiful wife, a jet, and a pretty healthy bank account."

You can imagine how surprised the two friends were when they ran into him six months later. He was wearing a polyester leisure suit and was working the night shift at a convenience store.

"What happened to you?" they both exclaimed.

"I loaned my yacht to a friend and he ran it aground. It sank, and I had no insurance."

"Hell," said one of the friends, "it's only a boat."

"Yes, but I didn't have insurance on my plane either, and it was destroyed in a fire in the hangar."

"Hey, take heart," said the other friend, "at least you have your lovely wife and your money."

"Not so fast, fellas," moaned the poor salesman. "My wife ditched me for another guy, her lawyer took me for every cent I had, and I was fired because I lost over half of my accounts. I'll tell you, though, I've learned one thing from all this: If it flies, floats, or fucks, lease it."

Weiss and Stein went into business together and opened up a wholesale men's clothing outlet. Things went well for a year or so, but then the recession came along and they found themselves sitting on ten thousand Madras jackets which they couldn't sell to save their souls. Just as they were discussing bankruptcy, a fellow came in and introduced himself as a buyer for a big menswear line in Australia. "Wouldn't happen to have any Madras jackets, would you?" he asked. "They're selling like crazy down under."

Weiss looked at Stein. "Maybe we can work something out, if the price is right," he said coolly.

After some tough negotiating a price was agreed on and the papers signed. But as he was leaving, the Australian said, "Just one thing, mates: I've got to get authorization from the home office for a deal this big. Today's Monday; if you don't get a cable from me by Friday, the deal's final."

For the next four days, Stein and Weiss paced miserably back and forth, sweating bullets and wincing every time they heard footsteps outside their door. On Friday the hours crept by, but by four o'clock they figured they were home free—until there was a loud knock on the door. "Western Union!" a voice called out.

As Stein collapsed, white-faced, behind his desk, Weiss dashed to the door. A minute later, he rushed back in waving a telegram. "Great

114

news, Stein," he cried jubilantly, "great news! Your mother's dead!"

•

Stuart Jefferson is having a party to celebrate his new promotion as divisional sales manager for International Harvester. "You know," he laments to his guests, "over the past year, I've sold more diesel shovels and back hoes than anyone in the history of the company, but do they call me Stu the Super Salesman? No.

"And recently I've volunteered hundreds of hours to various charities and causes around the city, but am I called Stu the Concerned Citizen? No, sir.

"But suck one little cock . . ."

•

A travelling salesman drove into a filling station in his fancy Cadillac. The blonde pump girl noticed some of his golfing equipment on the front seat, and asked the driver about it. So the salesman good-naturedly explained, "Those are my tees—I rest my balls on them when I drive."

"Gee whiz!" exclaimed the blonde, "what'll those Cadillac makers think of next?"

Why are salesmen so jealous of prostitutes?
  "Ya got it, ya sell it, ya still got it."

•

Three young women were hired by a large elec-
tronics firm on the same day. A year later the
sales manager of the company said each was due
for a promotion, and that each would get her
own office with her name on the door.

One day one of the women came in and found
to her surprise and dismay that the other two
had already moved into their own offices. Going
into the sales manager's office, she asked when
her office would be ready.

The sales manager pushed back his chair from
his desk and unzipped his fly. "See this?" he
asked. "This is quality. And in this company,
quality goes in before the name goes on."

•

A yuppie salesman was informed that the recession was really hurting business, and that the
company was enforcing a 30% cut in pay. Later
that evening he broke the bad news to his wife,

and they started discussing how they could trim their budget.

"Honey," he proposed rather snidely, "if you could learn to prepare a few meals, we could let the cook go."

"Well, dear," she replied, "if you could learn to fuck, we could fire the gardener."

•

The sales manager of a factory that made rubber goods, from tires to rubber bands, was giving some potential customers a tour. Of special interest was the condom plant, where rubbers were being peeled off cock-shaped molds and rolled up for packaging. But every twelfth one was shuttled aside and a small hole was punched in it. Shocked, one of the customers exclaimed, "What are you doing? Think of all the unwanted pregnancies that's going to cause!"

"Yes," agreed the sales manager, "but it sure boosts sales in the nipple division."

•

Mr. Cohen emigrates to the United States as a young man and fulfills the immigrant's dream: he starts up his own nail factory in Brooklyn, expands and profits, buys a nice house on Long

Island, sends his kids to college, even puts the older son through Harvard Business School. When the young man graduates, Mr. Cohen says to him, "Moishe, you're a smart one. I'm going to turn the business over to you and retire to Miami Beach."

A year later he gets an excited call from Moishe. "Dad. Things are going great. I've computerized inventory, automated the factory, even got a great new ad campaign going. Sales are gonna skyrocket, I'm telling you. You've gotta come see it with your own eyes."

So he picks his dad up at the airport, and just before they get off the expressway at the factory exit, a huge billboard looms up. It's a close-up of Jesus on the cross, with the slogan, USE COHEN'S NAILS FOR THE TOUGHEST JOBS.

"Oy, Moishe," groans Cohen, *"that's* your new campaign? I'm tellin' you, the goys are never gonna go for it."

A year later Moishe calls again. "Dad, Dad, things are going great, you gotta come up and see for yourself. And by the way, you were right about that ad campaign; we've got a whole new one going now."

So again Cohen gets on a plane and again Moishe picks him up at the airport. And there's the same huge billboard, only this time the picture shows Jesus in a heap at the foot of the cross and the slogan reads YOU SHOULDA USED CO-HEN'S NAILS.

•

First salesman: "I made some very valuable contacts today."
Second salesman: "I didn't get any orders, either."

•

The Arab sheik welcomed his son back from a tour of the United States, and was eager for the young man's opinions of the place. "What impressed you the most, Fouad?" he pressed eagerly. "The natural resources? The lush scenery? Maybe the blonde women? The democratic system at work? Or perhaps by the Americans' freedom from class distinctions, by their energy and initiative?"

"To tell you the truth, Dad," replied the prince, unpacking six pairs of snowshoes, "what impressed me the most was their salesmanship."

Would you like to see your favorite tasteless jokes in print? If so, send them to:

Blanche Knott
c/o St. Martin's Press
175 Fifth Avenue
New York, N.Y. 10010

I'm sorry, but no compensation or credit can be given. But I *love* hearing from my tasteless readers.

- If the mistake is in your favor, don't correct it.
- Cut people off in the middle of their sentences.
- Turn on your brights for oncoming traffic.
- Develop a convenient memory.
- Take personal calls during important meetings.
- Carve your name in picnic tables.
- Don't leave a message at the beep.
- Leave your supermarket cart on the street or in the parking lot.
- Ask her if the diamond ring is real.
- Before exiting the elevator, push all the buttons.

These and 502 more boorish, insensitive and socially obnoxious pointers for leading a simple, self-centered life may be found in

# Life's Little Destruction Book
## A Parody

### A Stonesong Press Book by
### Charles Sherwood Dane
### Available from St. Martin's Press